THE MISS

MW00490051

A Human Approach To Creating a Healthy Workplace Culture

Where Great People Love to Come to Work, Feel Safe, Respected,

Valued, Supported, and Empowered

Videos at: samglenn.com

Sam Glenn

Award Winning Speaker, Best Selling Author, and

Inspirational Artist

Published by Sam Glenn, Inc. 2014 / 2019

ebook/2022 ISBN 978-969-2592-22-2

Table Of Contents

Sam Glenn

"When you grow your people, your people grow your organization."

The Culture Test

- If I spent one day working for you or with you, would I want to come back the next day?

- If I randomly asked anyone within your organization, "How is it working here?" Would the majority of what they share be good or or not so good?

- On a scale of 1-10, 10 being the most. How well do your people feel supported, recognized, respected, valued, safe, motivated, inspired, challenged, growing, and driven by purpose? _____

- Is your organization more of a home for renters or for long term home buyers?

- On a scale of 1-10, 10 being the most. How well does your leadership demonstrate they care and support others?

Allow Me to Introduce Myself

My name is Sam Glenn. I work with organizations and leaders around the globe helping to equip them to create healthy, safe, and empowering workplace cultures. Basically, I help organizations find, restore, rekindle, and feed that spark of excellence that makes going to work rewarding, fulfilling, and profitable.

My expertise is based around what drives everything we know our attitude. I have published more than 56 books over the span of two decades. Every bit of research and study, as well as real-life observations and experiences I have had, points to attitude as the main driver of both our actions and our choices. From a metrics standpoint, it is our EI or EQ (emotional intelligence) that has the greatest influence in driving our IQ (intelligence quotient). If there is one simple, yet incredible truth about this thing called attitude, it's that only we can choose it, everything follows it, and it will change everything. Your attitude is your brand, your logo, your culture, your service, your leadership, and ultimately your legacy.

Remember, your attitude is not a soft skill, it is a human and life skill. It is either your greatest asset or your biggest liability. If your attitude isn't working for you or your organization, don't expect anything at all to work right. Please keep in mind, this isn't a book about positivity. I don't give talks or speak on positivity. Positivity is a reward you give yourself and others for choosing to think better. When we think better, we lead better, communicate better, handle change or setbacks better, and are just better people all around. Things only get better as much as we do.

MY CHALLENGE TO YOU

While there are tons of outstanding books on building a better workplace culture and improving your leadership performance, I want to highlight a few key points that really don't get covered much, however they tend to have the most significant impact. My mission is to support your leadership efforts from a human standpoint and share what I have seen that works and the most common things that just do not work. When I say human, I mean exactly what I am saying, "You demonstrate humanness towards other humans." When you see people as more than workers or numbers, your approach in how you lead changes significantly. When your approach changes, so do your outcomes.

So, my challenge to you, as you read this book, is to find ONE GOOD IDEA that will contribute to the betterment of your organization and leadership. I am confident that if you get one good idea from this book and implement it, that simple change will have the power to change everything. I see it happen every day. Your attitude and approach should be to look for something good each day that will make things good or better yet significantly better. Again, your culture and leadership will only improve as much as you get better yourself.

FIND ONE GOOD IDEA that will contribute to the betterment of your organization and leadership. One good idea has the potential to change everything! And that's a very good thing.

The Spark

It all Starts with this and

Everything Follows it

It is not what everyone knows how to do, trained to do, or educated and experienced to do, but rather the "SPARK" behind what they do. The Spark is excellence, support, respect, safety, enthusiasm, purpose, integrity, empathy, encouragement, mentorship, inclusion, diversity, motivation, joy, fulfillment, teamwork, and more.

The spark is what fuels your workplace culture. A workplace should not be a place that makes people FEEL sick, afraid, depressed, hopeless, uncaring, forgotten, invisible, or uninspired. When the spark is missing, it is evident in communication, service experiences, quality of product, ethics, and the bottom line—whatever that might be for you.

REMEMBER

"EXCELLENCE IS NOT AN

ACCIDENT."

In the next few pages, I am going to share some very simple ideas that have the potential to transform your workplace culture in the best ways possible. These ideas absolutely work—I have countless emails from leaders in every state who share how well they have worked and are working for their organization every day! Most of the leadership teams who hire me already have outstanding workplace cultures, some of the very best, so even if you feel you already have a great culture, it has the potential to keep getting better. Many of my clients have even been honored with being rated one of the best places to work in their industry, state, or country. So, you might wonder if they are already achieving excellence, why work with someone like me or read a book on improving you culture? That's a good question. Think about it from this perspective, why do you get an oil change for your car every 5,000 miles? Why do you charge your phone every day? Why does a super bowl championship team hire someone, who has never played a single game, to speak and inspire the team before game time?

I like to think of it as supporting momentum in the right direction. In fact, a few years back, I had just finished speaking at an HR Conference and two weeks after the meeting, one of the attendees emailed me, "Sam, your speech was incredible. It has been a long time that I have felt that good about myself and my work. But I noticed that it has been two weeks since I heard you speak, and the fire has burned out. I feel blah again. What can I do?"

He said it, "The fire has burned out." It's like going camping, you can start a fire, but it is up to you to take ownership of that fire and do the things that it takes to keep it going. If your fire burns out it is because either you let it burn out or you did not protect it from external sources that caused it to burn out. We all get burned out from time to time, but like a lightbulb that burns out, I can complain about it, blame someone about it, make drama about it, or I can just take immediate action and change the light bulb myself for a new one that works.

If you are winning, you want the winning streak to continue. One observation about organizations that struggle with creating an engaged culture is that they actively choose to NOT invest in their people in the right ways. They do not find value in investing in creating a thriving safe, respectful, and supportive workplace culture. Their viewpoint is that everything is a potentially unneeded expense, rather than an investment. So instead of choosing to invest in their people and culture the right way they prioritize eliminating or minimizing expenses for the sake of monetary profit. They do not understand what that "profit" is actually costing them and their team members.

Let me be clear when I say, there is a reason why winning teams win. They do what it takes each day to win—they choose to win. I heard a quote the other day that speaks volumes, "If you think the price of winning is too expensive, wait until you get the bill for regret."

Makes you think.

In this book, I am going to focus more on the human aspect of creating a better workplace culture. This is not a technical or tactical approach; this is a book about being human toward other humans. In this book I will dismantle the belief that attitude is a "soft skill." There are no such thing as soft skills. Someone made it up and the definition expanded. There are only human skills and life skills. These are the drivers of our abilities, talents, education, expertise, experiences, and knowledge. It doesn't matter if everyone riding in your car or bus is smart, educated, and talented, if the driver is not equipped or does not possess those abilities, you will never reach the right destination.

It Doesn't Matter How Much You Know, Unless it is Supported by this One Little Thing

A CFO said to the CEO, "What if we invest in our people and they leave?'

The CEO responded by saying, "What if we don't invest in our people and they stay?"

It all starts with this one little thing—ATTITUDE!

I am sure you have heard the saying, "I don't care how much you know, until I know how much you care." That statement could not be truer when it comes to creating a culture of engagement. Caring is a human expression of giving intentional thought and consideration to another person. This is also the very point where TRUST is built.

And once you have established trust with another person, others will trust what you know.

Over the past 27 years, I have had the opportunity to work with leadership in quite literally every type of industry you can imagine—software, healthcare, medical, education, insurance, government, professional sports, automotive, agriculture, property management, animal science, retail, construction, administration, maintenance—you name it! If there is one common thread that stands out the most when leaders hire me to speak at their meetings or conferences, it is that they actively care about their people. They don't just say, "We care" or put it on their website or a t-shirt. They live it each day and it is obvious! They walk the talk and that is impressive.

These leaders understand that the achievement of recognition as well as attaining the right results can only happen when you have the right people doing the right things, the right way. They know that they need team members with the right attitude and who are functioning within the right environment. They ensure that their people are valued, supported, heard, respected, empowered, growing, and safe—not just occasionally, but daily and consistently.

The reason I am so passionate about helping others improve their workplace culture is because growing up, I never saw my parents come home from any job happy. A good leader has awareness and understands that work has a significant impact on a person's home and personal life. My parents worked hard, but they never sang the praises of the organizations they worked for—EVER! They never said, "I work for great people or a great organization. I would never consider looking for another job."

When your parents look defeated and exhausted by working within an organization that doesn't care about their people, it affects you. It affected me. Nobody should go to work and feel worse or bad about their life. I happen to believe that any job has the potential to be both fulfilling and rewarding. It can and should be more than just a job, it can become both an opportunity and a blessing.

The focus of this short book is to supplement your attitude with a little extra strength, optimism, and resilience. As an engaging leader, you need these tools working for you. This book is about acknowledging and developing your humanness so you can treat other people with kindness, dignity, respect, and bring out the best in them. Because at the end of the day, that is what it is all about.

Aristotle said it best, "Educating the mind without educating the heart is no education at all."

Let's dive in...

Value Progress Over Perfection

One of the biggest complaints I hear most often from leaders is how challenging it can be to improve employee engagement within their workplace. It has become a hot topic, but also one that many leaders overthink and overcomplicate. Let me very clear when I say this, "Creating engagement in the workplace does not have to be difficult and never should be."

Improving your culture starts by improving your engagement strategies. This is a process of progression, not perfection. It's a process of learning and growing. It's gathering honest feedback, and then using that feedback to make positive changes. It is crucial to remember you need people to feel safe sharing feedback with you. If you exist in an echo chamber of people just telling you that you are doing a great job or who feel so ambivalent towards you or their job that they just don't see the point in sharing honest feedback, you will never be able to grow, improve yourself, and create a better culture. When people do not feel safe sharing honest feedback, you will either be left guessing or waste time, money, and resources on things that don't have any relevant meaning to your team. This means asking the question, "What can I do better that would be helpful to you?" or "What can we do better as an organization that would improve your experience working here?"

Don't get offended by the feedback or take it personally, but rather use it and be inspired by it. When people see you listening to their feedback and then making positive changes they will be inspired to work harder and get better themselves. Sometimes they will share feedback about something that you are not able to change, and in those situations, you have the opportunity to share the "why" behind why a certain policy or procedure is in place. Or, through open and transparent dialogue, you might discover there is a way to keep that policy and procedure in place but improve it or make it less of a burden.

At the time of writing this, there is a massive teacher shortage across the country. What happened? Did teachers just stop caring and lose interest in teaching? No way! Every August, I crisscross the nation speaking at opening days for schools. Thousands of teachers make their way back to prepare for a new school year and start their year in the most positive ways possible. Not a single school I have spoken at in the past three years (even during the pandemic) have experienced staffing or teacher shortage issues. So, what's the difference?

The biggest difference is the leadership of these schools is diligent and intentional about creating a culture that attracts and retains great teachers.

How many of you have seen signs in local businesses that say, "Please be patient with us, we have a staffing shortage?"

If you ever see a sign like that, it's pretty much a very strong indication that the business or organization has not created a culture that attracts and retains great people.

Recently, I had to find a new printer to assist with my printing needs. My old printer was awesome. They were responsive by email, in person, and on the phone. I was always so impressed with the results they provided me as the customer. However, one day, things changed. My emails were not being answered, nobody was returning my call, and when I showed up in person, there was a long line out the door. One early evening, I stopped in to ask, "What is going on or not going on?"

The young lady working there said, "All the good people left."

I was like, "What?!!!"

She didn't filter her words at all. She said, "I think I might go also. The management treats us so poorly here that everyone is leaving."

If you are not taking care of your people the way they deserve, they are going to go where they are celebrated and supported.

It was so disheartening because the people who normally helped me were "AMAZING!!!!!" They made their organization successful and look good. Yet, they were not appreciated or treated right, so they left. As a result, the business at this print location declined, they got more complaints and there it was—a sign, "Please be patient with us, we have a staffing shortage."

Please note, this is not giving people everything they want and turning your workplace into a free for all. Most of the ideas I am going to share with you do not even cost any money. Do not ever underestimate the power of simply treating people well and letting them know they are appreciated and valued members of the team. What they do matters, they make the organization better through their contributions and things would not be the same with out them. When you communicate these thoughts with people, they will want to do better work, contribute more effectively, and most importantly actually care about their work.

Let me share a few ideas so you never have to make a sign like that—EVER!

Improve Your Humanness

To create a more engaging workplace culture, you must remember that you are in the people business. If you work with people or even just one person, you are in the people business. What does this look like? This is showing a demonstration of decency, respect, and kindness to another person. Sounds simple, right? NOPE. This is the one point where people in leadership roles lose the entire game.

Several years ago, a close friend of our family was one of the top recruiters in the country. She was excellent at her job. She arrived ready to do her best each day and took a great deal of pride in her work. She was not always the "first one to arrive and last one to leave" each day but she worked diligently and made the most of each day seeking every opportunity to go above and beyond that she could. She maximized every opportunity she was given and always did her best to do "what's best for business." She brought in millions of dollars for her organization each year. However, one pay period there was a small error on her commission check, it was $1,000 short of what it should have been. When she asked her direct supervisor for assistance in fixing the error, his careless response was, "Just go with it, you should feel lucky you have a job during these times."

What he did not know at the time was that she was being actively recruited by their biggest competitor. They were offering more money, better opportunities for growth within the company, and the ability to work with bigger clients. Out of loyalty to the company she had been with for over 10 years she had been turning down the offers and was not even considering leaving at that point. That one careless sentence from her supervisor clearly communicated to her that she was not valued or appreciated. On her lunch break she stepped out and called the competitor and let them know she changed her mind and would be accepting the new position. When they asked why, she respectfully and truthfully explained what happened. The competitor understood and said that to demonstrate how different they are from her current company they would not just add $1,000 to her signing bonus to compensate for the other company's error but added $3,000 to her signing bonus because, as her new boss said, he was confident that they were "three times better than her current employer". She put in her two weeks' notice and that should be where the story ends. But instead of taking accountability for her leaving and learning from that experience, when the leadership team approached her supervisor about why she was leaving he said "Who knows? Some people just care about money, plus it's impossible to keep every good employee." He figured that was that and didn't think to mention that she had accepted a position with their largest competitor. Within her first two weeks at the new company, she closed three significant placements resulting in half a million dollars of profit for her new company. Apparently, her new boss has a sense of humor because he sent the leadership team at her old company a huge edible arrangement delivery, several thank you balloons, and a thoughtfully written thank you card. Let's just say her old supervisor was looking for a new job that afternoon.

Are you shaking your head also? That one disrespectful and thoughtless sentence cost the company millions in revenue all over a small, $1,000 mistake that could and should have been easily fixed. If people in leadership roles can't be decent, thoughtful, and supportive, they are just building doors that say EXIT HERE.

One of the most important lessons I took from this story is that you never know what is going on in a person's life if you do not actively demonstrate that you care for that person and listen to them. Because he did not care or value her as a team member, he shot off a single careless comment while having no idea what a huge gift he was giving his biggest competitor. The consequence or result of that one single sentence by our friend's direct supervisor not only cost the organization millions, but they let the supervisor go. He lost his job over one careless sentence. Which brings up a very good point, THINK BEFORE YOU SPEAK.

The key to humanness is how you treat "ALL PEOPLE," in person, virtually, on the phone or email. Let me ask you this, how do you treat the overly ambitious salesperson who contacts you every week and fills up your email inbox? Are you decent or rude to them? Or do you choose to follow the crowd and just ignore them?

If you cannot be human towards other people, then you need to fix something—YOU. You might argue, "Well Sam, I am super busy and don't have time for people who spam me weekly trying to sell me something I don't need."

I understand what busy is. I get it. However, wouldn't it be easier to create a system that allows you to make people feel seen, heard, and acknowledge them with decency?

If you don't have a system set up that helps you manage how to address spam or interruptions, then don't expect the situation to fix itself. The goal isn't just to make the people who profit feel valued, respected, and important, but anyone at all who encounters you. This is called branding. What is your total brand as a person and leader? If you are only decent to those who you think can be beneficial to you, you are like the person you take out for lunch and they are nice to you, but rude to the server. It doesn't matter what your title is or how much experience you have, if you cannot be decent toward others, meaning being human toward other humans, you may need to consider finding a new job. Engaging leadership is not about playing favorites but rooting for everyone to win.

Several years ago, I had an association executive blow up at me on email because speakers like me email him weekly and he was sick and tired of it. However, I don't tolerate or promote disrespect, so I called him out on his attitude. I asked him if it feels good being rude toward others because he doesn't have an effective system in place to manage people contacting him. I experience the same things that he experiences. My office gets hundreds of emails selling us stuff, asking questions like, "What is Sam's favorite color? What is Sam's story? How did he get started? Can you donate a speech? Books? Artwork? Can Sam give me advice on something?"

We do not just reply to emails or inquires that have the potential to profit my organization, but rather we have a system set up that makes every contact feel seen, heard, acknowledged, respected, and valued. When someone tries to sell me something that I don't need, I don't ignore them (like most people). I don't blast them for filling up my inbox. I acknowledge them with respect and let them know, "This isn't something I need right now but if anything changes, I will be sure to reach out to you first."

You can set boundaries and structure a system that allows you not to be distracted or disturbed by every request to interact with you, but rather is consistent with being human toward another human by offering decency, respect, and kindness. It also communicates that I understand what they do and if/when I need their services, I will approach them... so there is no need for continued marketing emails from them. I also do not respond to marketing emails as they come in, rather I set aside 10 minutes each day to respond to those emails. If an email comes in after that set time, then I do not respond to it until the set aside 10 minutes the following day.

When you are rooting for others, your approach changes, and what is required to make it effective is consistency and kindness.

My branding is so consistent that it has become easy and does not require much thought or effort on my part. I don't have to decide how to respond to each email and I don't become annoyed or frustrated by them. I know it will get taken care of during the set aside 10 minutes each day. So, what is your branding? If I email you today selling soap, would you ignore me, blast me, or be human towards me? What branding communicates you care? What branding makes your organization look good? What branding would make your family proud?

Think about this one for a bit. What do you want to be known for?

Are You Supporting Renters or Owners?

Does your culture support renters or owners? Think about it, if people are coming to work and looking for a better gig on their lunch break, that means you have renters. Eventually, they will leave for a better gig. They are not all in. They don't feel valued, supported, or like they have the potential to grow, so they are working under the distraction of looking for a better deal. However, if you have people who come to work and love their work and are confident that their contributions are essential for the organization's success, that means you are supporting an ownership mentality. You are choosing to do something to create a place where there are no other tempting options or better deals.

Renters are expensive because unnecessary turnover is like flushing good money down the drain. If your turnover is significant, that is a red flag that something is not right on the most basic level. Your mission as an engaged leader is to cultivate an ownership mentality. To do this you must demonstrate an ownership mentality. This requires taking an honest evaluation of your thoughts and actions. If you see a piece of trash on the floor, do you pick it up or do you assume that "whoever's job is to clean the place will pick it up."

I want to introduce Walmart Fred. I was checking out of Walmart not too long ago and normally you really don't see employees smiling at Walmart. That is not a dig towards Walmart, but it's true. I've noticed any time I have gone into any Walmart, regardless of the city or state, you really do not see employees displaying joy or happiness. Walmart has two big things going for them that will always keep them in business—cost and real estate. If they have that, they will always be in business. However, the customer experience at Walmart is a different story. The energy, positivity, and enthusiasm that Sam Walton envisioned for the organization has all but disappeared.

Every now and then you may experience a miracle. While I was in line to check out, I noticed the cashier's name was Fred. He looked to be in his 30's. He made eye contact with me. He even smiled a genuine smile at me. I thought maybe I was on a hidden camera show and briefly looked around to see if I could see any cameras. Then, to my surprise, he inquired as to how my day was going. So, I responded in kind, "Fred, my day is going well. How is your day going?"

Fred said something that displayed his driver—his attitude. He said, "It's a good day sir, I am so blessed to have this job!"

WOW!

You always have a choice on how you look at things. You can look at your job as a bust or a blessing. Fred saw the blessing. So, let's be real about Fred's job. It can be challenging, repetitive, and thankless. While the customer "may always be right" they are not always a joy to deal with. Some people complain, some people are just plain angry, and many people do not even look up from their phone and acknowledge Fred during their brief exchange.

I think Fred found something in his work that made his job much more than just a paycheck. He had purpose, he believed he had potential for growth within the company, and he felt valued. When you have those three things working for you, your job is not just work, it's an opportunity and privilege. Fred may not have the most glamorous job in the world, but he makes the best of that job and that is what makes him stand out and as a result, make Walmart look good.

Would you give Fred a round of applause?!

Stick to the Fundamentals

When I played sports, the coach or leader of the team always stressed one key point, "Stick to the FUNDAMENTALS."

Fundamentals serve as the groundwork and foundation of a mission or purpose. If the fundamentals are not firm in your culture, there will be cracks in your foundation and wherever cracks show up, there are consequences.

Before I graduated from college, I had an opportunity to do an internship with a certain company that was rated number one at the time within their industry. When our university had job fairs, there was a line a mile long of students who wanted to work for this company. Everyone believed if you got their name on your resume, you could write your ticket anywhere. That is how much clout this organization carried at the time.

41

On average, they might hire two students from our university each year. Just two! The year before I graduated, I was one of them. Honestly, I think the fact that I made the person interviewing me laugh is what helped me get a foot in the door. She even said, "Wow, I haven't laughed like that in forever." She then communicated how much she liked my attitude and how this massive organization would benefit from someone with such a cheerful attitude.

Was I smarter than the hundreds of students lined up for a chance to work for this powerhouse of a company? Nope. In fact, if there were 300 in my class, I am pretty sure I would have graduated 301. It was proof that the partnership of the right attitude and the right skills opens doors more often than not. My fellow classmates felt entitled based on their level of education. I felt grateful. They relied on what they knew. I relied on what I could put behind what I knew. The outcome, I got the job and they had to keep searching. Instead of accepting a full-time position, I requested an internship first to see if it would be something I would want to do full time.

Here is where the story takes a turn. I had assumed that since this was the biggest and most prestigious organization in the world in their industry, that I would be working with some of the best people in the world. Talk about a disappointing first day. I am an observer by nature and what I observed was not good. I observed how people answered the phone—rudely. I observed how managers talked down to employees. I observed how people cut corners and justified their actions because they were not getting paid enough to care. I observed a morale so low that I wondered if everyone had just come to work from a funeral.

When I got back to my dorm on campus, everyone stopped by to ask me how it went. I was depressed. I said to everyone who asked me about working there, "The next time the university has a job fair, do not get in that line. Trust me, do not get in that line to interview for that company."

I wanted to quit every day. An engaged workplace culture shouldn't make people want to give up. I didn't realize how creative of a person I was until I had to come up with excuses as to why I couldn't make it into work. Basically, I was just trying to protect my wellbeing. I got physically sick knowing I had to go to this place of work. But regardless of how I felt I went in each day hoping for the best but prepared for the worst. I worked to the best of my ability, I worked to complete my tasks not just on time but early. Slowly though I noticed that I didn't like who I was or how I felt while I was there each day. I found myself becoming like my environment. This story has a happy ending—for me that is. At the end of my internship, they recognized my hard work, and they offered me a full-time position with a very nice salary, but I passed. Everyone thought I was crazy for passing up what they perceived to be a huge opportunity with generous compensation. I knew that in the end, they would just be paying me to be stressed, unhappy, and miserable. I couldn't do that, I didn't want that. This organization created a false perception of who they really were. They got you in the door, but they didn't know how to keep the good ones long term.

So, I should probably point out, what built this organization up to being the highest rated organization in its industry were fundamentals. What caused its downfall, was a gradual lack of attention to the fundamentals and shifting priorities. The cracks in the foundation became too great and this giant of a company previously known around the world for being the best came crashing down. This company no longer exists. The moral of the story, stick to the fundamentals of what creates success, support them daily, and maintain the right focus and priorities.

Lead by Example

"I hope this sucker burns!"

Yep, that is what I heard echo as hundreds of people were exiting a building that they thought was on fire. I was on the 25th floor of a skyscraper in Chicago consulting with a group that wanted to improve their workplace engagement. We had been in their conference room for about two hours when the fire alarm went off. We were asked to make our way down the stairs, and I heard someone say many times, "I hope this sucker burns!"

Not the most inspiring words you want to hear during an emergency. However, the guy behind me started laughing. I inquired, "What is so funny?"

He responded, "That's the leader of our company."

"Ohhhh nooooo!"

Now, I understood why they asked me to help their organization improve their workplace culture. However, an organization or a team only gets better as much as their people get better. I can offer ideas, but if you won't do the work to implement them, then we are just spinning our wheels and wasting the most precious gift we have on this planet—TIME.

Your example is literally your greatest influence. It communicates what you are about. It is the partnership of your attitude and actions. It is how you respond to setbacks. It is how you manage conflict. It is how you treat others. Your example is in everything. Whatever example you create, others will replicate. If your example lacks integrity, you can expect others to replicate a lack of integrity.

The goal should always be refining your example. The way you do that is to strive to get better each day. As humbling as you might feel it is, what do you need to improve on or work on that will refine the quality of your example?

Make little edits daily. Allow those edits to add up and create an example that truly makes life better for yourself and others.

Recognize, Reward, and Reinforce Greatness

I've never met anyone who left or quit a job because they felt over appreciated. Have you?

When someone does something good, tell them. It doesn't have to be a production or an annual event for it to happen. Just a few authentic, simple, and powerful words, thank you!

It was May 29, 1953 when Sir Edmond Hillary was credited with reaching the summit of Mount Everest. When he was being interviewed by the press about how he felt to be the first human to reach the summit, he acknowledged that it was a team effort. He said, "There were over 200 people involved in this expedition. In order to reach the summit, everyone had to play their part."

He gave the credit away.

If you see someone doing something that is helpful and good for the organization, tell them. Praise them. If you are a leader who loves to give gifts as rewards, do it! Probably my favorite story is one leader who bought his entire team a house cleaning service for a year. Do you know what feels amazing at the end of a long and hard workday? Going home to a clean house! What an amazing gift. This was not just a gift to his team though. He chose a local, small family-owned cleaning service known for their great work and quickly became their biggest customer.

It's important to know that recognition and rewards do not always have to be an expense. Some people just want to know that they matter, that they are seen, and their work is valued. The two most powerful words any leader can say to cultivate engagement on a budget are, "THANK YOU."

Just say thank you. When you "AUTHENTICALLY" communicate gratitude, it communicates that you are looking for things to be thankful for, and you notice and see their hard work.

Set Your People up for

Success

An engaged leader is one who focuses on setting others up for success. When organizations hire me to speak, they contact my team to discuss their event, and together we determine if my speech is a good fit for their organization. The first thing we look for is ATTITUDE. If someone is excited about my content and having me as a speaker, they go out of their way to set me up for success because they know it will create success and energy for their event.

My booking manager is always paying attention to a few things during the initial call. Their attitude towards the event, if they see value in my presentation, and how they treat what they perceive to be a person in a lower position than themselves. If they are rude to my admin that is a great indicator that they are rude to their own staff. Regardless of what they are willing to pay, we will turn down that business every single time. We are never desperate for anyone's business, but we are always ready and excited for the right business. Part of what my team does is ensuring that I am going into a situation where I am set up for success and will be speaking for people who want me there. They know that if I am set up for success, it will be a successful event and the client will have an awesome experience. And when the event is over, I will have peace of mind about the experience, and the client will have had an unforgettable positive experience.

We have had to learn a few lessons to get to this point though. Years ago, I was speaking at an event in Minnesota and part of the experience I create for others is painting a picture during my speech. I am a visual learner and I noticed that most meetings are filled with unremarkable PowerPoint presentations, so I try to provide a break from that and do something more engaging, creative, and memorable.

The only things we ask our clients to provide for my speech are a large canvas (five foot canvases are not very practical to fly with), a few drop clothes, and a small table and chairs. Well, I showed up to the venue ready to set up, and my client said she didn't have any of the supplies. Her reasoning was, "I didn't think they were that important."

I was like, "What?"

"I didn't think you needed them. You're just giving a speech, right?"

I felt my stomach drop because someone made a choice that didn't set me up for success. It was frustrating and disappointing. That decision cheated their entire organization out of an unforgettable experience, and they did not get the full value of their investment in my keynote. From that point on, we decided to only work with those organizations and leaders who share the same value of setting others up for success.

If you have ever seen an episode of Undercover Boss, it focuses on a similar concept. A leader or executive goes undercover to learn about what is working and what isn't working within their organization. In the process they get to know the stories of their employees, people they had never taken the time to get to know before and look for ways to remove limitations and set each team member up for greater success.

Embrace Your Mistakes

Most people do not wake up with the intention to fail and disappoint. However, mistakes and failure can be incredibly valuable. Does it feel good? Nope, not in the moment! But mistakes are a part of the process of engaging leadership. If you keep making the same mistake repeatedly, then you are not learning the lesson. However, if a mistake makes you better, wiser and sharper, then that is valuable.

Do you know the one thing that prevents an average leader from becoming an exceptional leader? Their ability to make mistakes and use them. The fear of making mistakes keeps more leaders from being great leaders than any other thing.

"What if it doesn't work?"

"What if I look foolish?"

"What if nobody likes it?"

"What if I get made fun of?

You will drain all of your leadership power when you:

1. Revisit and dwell on past mistakes.

2. Try to control what is outside your control.

3. Worry about the future.

4. Compare yourself to others.

5. Over prioritize the things that don't matter.

6. Treat everything like an emergency.

7. Micromanage your team.

8. Fail to empower your team to work independently.

Doing nothing is so much worse than doing something.

One day, Albert Einstein was teaching his class and wrote on the board,

9 x 1 = 9

9 x 2 = 18

9 x 3 = 27

He continued all the way up to 9 x 10 = 91

The class broke out in laughter because Einstein made a mistake. Obviously, the correct answer was 9 x 10 = 90. However, the students laughed at him.

Einstein waited for everyone to be silent and said, "Despite the fact that I analyzed nine problems correctly, no one congratulated me. But, when I made one mistake, everyone started laughing. This means even if a person is successful, society will notice even the slightest mistake."

Mistakes are part of the process. Learn from them. Grow from them. Use them as steppingstones. In the words of Albert Einstein, "The only person who never makes a mistake is someone who does nothing."

The Keeper of the Spring

Many times, when it's a matter of the heart or attitude, we shy away from that element because we don't know how to measure it. How do you put a metric on enthusiasm, inspiration, and purpose?

Years ago, I arrived to give a speech and my clients were so excited to have me kick off their all-employee function. When I arrived, I was informed that they had been trying to get me to speak to their employees for over six years. However, the reason it never happened was the CEO. For six years, he believed that the morale was low, turnover was on the rise, and engagement was at an all time low. Their idea was to take a break, do something special for everyone, recognize them, and encourage them. However, the CEO kept putting it off and his reasoning was, "We are here to work and get a job done. Once this next project is complete, we can do something."

He kept procrastinating wellness. He put off what would help. Think about it this way, if I gave you a dull razor, would you trust that dull razor to do its job properly? NO WAY! A dull razor carries with it a pricy and painful consequence. Trust me, I KNOW! The question is, "Is it really worth it?" Are you really willing to use a dull razor and expect excellent results?

It would seem like common sense not to use a dull razor, however, here is some truth—common sense isn't a common practice. Let me ask you this, when is the best time to inspire or cheer someone on who is running a marathon? Before the race, during the race, or after the race? The answer is before, during, and after.

Inspiration isn't a touchy-feely thing. It is food for purpose. Without inspiration, there is no connection to our purpose. Enthusiasm dwindles. Without inspiration, we are like a campfire without a spark—it doesn't work. We become work zombies. A work zombie does what they know how to do and what they get paid to do. Nothing more. Nothing less. There is no life or passion in their work. It reminds me of the two janitors mopping floors at NASA. Both were asked how their days were going. The first janitor responded, "New day, same old thing."

The second janitor replied, "It is going FANTASTIC! We are sending people to outer space!"

What was the difference? ATTITUDE.

One did his work because it was his job. He was a work zombie.

The other was connected to the big picture, so he had purpose in his work. He wasn't just mopping floors, he was an important part of sending people into outer space. He believed his role on the team was to keep the floors clean and safe to walk on. He knew that if he did not do his job properly someone else on the team could slip, fall, and get hurt, and that would put the entire mission at risk. He took his job just as seriously as the engineers and astronauts did.

So back to my story. As I was doing my sound check for this all-employee event, I was informed that the CEO had retired two weeks prior and that the new CEO's first order of business was to do something special for everyone, to recharge their batteries, celebrate them, and inspire them to reconnect to their purpose. I just happened to be part of the experience. Inspiration can be a powerful tool. Think about it this way, do you by chance watch sports? I personally love watching football, specifically NFL football. Each player and coach has a clear understanding of what their role on the team is, performs it to the best of their ability, and are being compensated quite well to do their job. So why might they hire someone like me to speak to their organization? I have never played professional football or coached a team. But I am an expert at helping people connect with their purpose, do their jobs with excellence, and helping teams learn to treat each other well. They recognize the value of my message and know that while my experience is different than theirs, I can help them bring out the best in themselves and each other.

I want to share one of my absolute favorite stories and it highlights the value and importance of doing the little things that may not seem like a big deal in the moment but have the power to positively impact the trajectory of the entire team. This story is such a powerful example of that.

The Keeper of The Spring

The Keeper of the Spring was a quiet forest dweller who lived high above an Austrian village along the eastern slopes of the Alps. The old gentleman had been hired many years ago by a young town council team to clear away the debris from the pools of water up in the mountain crevices that fed the lovely spring flowing through their town. With faithful, silent regularity, he patrolled the hills, removed the leaves and branches, and wiped away the silt that would otherwise choke and contaminate the fresh flow of water. By and by, the village became a popular attraction for vacationers. Graceful swans floated along the crystal-clear spring, the millwheels of various businesses located near the water turned day and night, farmlands were naturally irrigated, and the view from restaurants was picturesque beyond description. Years passed. One evening the town council met for its semiannual meeting. As they reviewed the budget, one man's eye caught the salary being paid to the obscure keeper of the spring. Said the keeper of the purse, "Who is the old man? Why do we keep him on year after year? No one ever sees him. For all we know the stranger of the hills is doing us no good. He isn't necessary any longer!"

By a unanimous vote, they dispensed with the old man's services. For several weeks nothing changed. By early autumn the trees began to shed their leaves. Small branches snapped off and fell into the pools, hindering the rushing flow of sparkling water. One afternoon someone noticed a slight yellowish-brown tinting the spring. A couple days later the water was much darker. Within one week, the water was along the banks and a foul odor was soon detected. The millwheels moved slower, some finally ground to a halt. Swans left as did the tourists. Clammy fingers of disease and sickness reached deeply into the village. Quickly, the embarrassed council called a special meeting. Realizing their gross error in judgment, they hired back the old keeper of the spring... and within a few weeks the veritable river of life began to clear up. The wheels started to turn, and new life returned to the hamlet in the Alps once again.

If you reread The Keep of the Spring a few times, it will sink in big time! It is so powerful.

Get Out of the Way

Micromanagement is a death sentence to any success of an organization. If you are micromanaging your people, you are communicating, "I do not trust you."

And if you are micromanaging because they are not living up to the agreed expectations of work, then why are they still there renting space?

The best advice I have for engaging leaders is get out of the way and allow people to do what they have been hired to do. If they need support or mentorship, make that available, but don't be breathing down someone's neck while they work. You will make them and yourself crazy.

I remember during the pandemic, I was doing several virtual shows a week, and they were awesome. We had an emcee and gave away incredible prizes during each show. We made the best of what wasn't the best and it all turned out for the best.

One day, I received an email from someone who explained that their company was "always" changing ownership and that it was stressful. There was more to the story, and I always like to help when I can. So, this person had to sell me to her leadership. She said she had to bend over backwards to get them to say yes and at a reduced fee. Normally, I would have passed, but I wanted to support this person. (Allow me to pause for a moment and point something out, if you must bend over backwards to sell a speech that empowers your people to think and do better, something is very wrong. This is why organizations that have poor cultures do not hire me often. They don't get it. They see my speech as an expense not an investment into their people).

When we set up the customization call with their leadership, it lasted over an hour. My keynote virtual session that they wanted was only 30 minutes. But they required over an hour of my time just to communicate what they wanted, and even at that they were not even on the same page. They had five people in different leadership roles on the call and it literally felt like a bus of kids at a fast-food drive through as they were all shouting over each other what they wanted. Each leader was only focused on their individual team and what they wanted their individual team to take a way. There was no consideration as to what would be best for the organization as a whole. It was abundantly clear that they were not a group of people who understood the concept of unity or what it means to all be working towards a common goal. I could clearly see why the person who contacted me was so stressed.

I had to coral them like a bunch of wild horses by asking for one word they could all agree on. I said, what is one word that is meaningful to your organization as a whole and would have a positive impact on your employees and their clients. It was almost comical the way they each used twenty plus words to communicate the one single word. They struggled with the simplicity of how simple I made things.

Finally, the head person asked if I could record my talk first and allow them to evaluate it and make changes for the

LIVE speech. To that my reply was a respectful but clear "NO."

Then I communicated some truth that I am pretty sure they didn't like, but is the very reason I almost always pass on events like this. It doesn't matter how great a job I do, they are going to look for and complain about everything that they perceive is "wrong." If I use the word one of the leaders gave me then the other four leaders would feel like my message does not apply to them and disregard it. Their lack of awareness was so apparent that I am guessing if they ever did read this book, they would not even realize this story is about their specific organization. If I asked them for a review of this book, they would find everything they didn't like about the book and share that with everyone. An encouraging leader might notice something they perceive to be wrong, but they will always seek to highlight what is right and share positivity and encouragement with others. Do you see the difference?

I said, "It is honor to speak at your event. I have a great speech customized for your event that will make you look good and that you will be proud to have shared with your team. The lesson here is you must allow me to do what I do best and what you have hired me to do. That means, having a little faith and trusting that I am capable of not just meeting your expectations but exceeding them. You can't control everything and expect the best results or for anything to change in a positive direction. Sometimes, the best thing you can do to allow people to thrive and be successful is to get out of the way and let them shine."

The day of the virtual show arrived, and my team was ready to go. We logged in and watched about an hour of their virtual conference before my closing. First, they said they were expecting 500 people to participate. Less than 70 showed up. As we watched the sessions, you could tell that each presenter was carefully micromanaged. They were like robots. They lacked emotion, feeling, and connection. They were humans doing what they were told to do. There was nothing natural about it. It was so forced and unnatural that I was seriously questioning if they were reading a teleprompter at gunpoint.

When I was introduced, I was literally given the absolute worst introduction on the planet. They did not set me up for success. All they said was, "And now here is Sam." That was it! There was no build up, excitement, energy, life, or reason to stay glued to your screen in the middle of the day for 30 more minutes. The irony of the fact that they tried to micromanage everything about my speech but failed to do the one thing I asked them to do (read the introduction that they were sent) was not lost on me.

Initially, I was like a deer in headlights due to the shock of such a terrible introduction. However, my team are masters at improv, so our emcee took the mic and redid the introduction, which was EPIC! By the time he finished the introduction, even I was excited to hear me speak. The session went incredibly. I found out later that when they did the evaluations, my session stole the show and received the highest evaluations out of all the sessions. Of course, it did—we made it so it would. But, most of all, I established a boundary that allowed me to be my natural best. I was the only presenter that was allowed to be his natural best because I wasn't micromanaged.

Getting out of the way doesn't mean you disappear. You check in and ask, "Do you need anything? Can I do anything to help? Is there anything I can do to better equip you to complete this? How is it going? Do you feel like you will complete this task on time, or do you think it might require more or less time?" Just note, please do not ask them all these questions a once... one or two at a time will do the trick.

You are there to support their success and help them achieve the established expectations, but you cannot and should not do it for them. They might not be doing it the way you would do it... but you were not hired to do their job. You were hired to equip them and support them in doing their job. You must let them do what they do best.

Sam Glenn

There are ONLY Two Types of Leaders, Which One are You?

In my 27 years of research and studying leaders on paper and in person, I have noticed that there really are only two types of Leaders. There are Rooters and there are Looters.

- Yep, Rooters and Looters.

- Let me break it down for you.

- A Rooter looks out for others.

- A Looter looks out for themselves.

- A Rooter looks for solutions.

- A Looter makes excuses.

- A Rooter accepts responsibility.

- A Looter accepts a paycheck and does the minimum required to accomplish their tasks.

- Rooters say, "THANK YOU."

- Looters feel ENTITELED.

- A Rooter empowers others.

- A Looter blames others.

- A Looter makes work more difficult.

- A Rooter will try new things.

- A Looter will play it safe.

- A Rooter thinks better.

- A Looter thinks the same.

- A Rooter gives credit.

- A Looter takes credit.

- I think you get the idea.

Not so long ago, I was doing a book signing after giving two different speeches and I was able to observe both types of leaders. The first event, the CEO was not very personable. When he got up to speak, he basically thanked himself and tried to make himself look good for his choices and leadership abilities. In fact, before the event, they asked if during my speech, I would paint a picture of him... not for him... of him, my quick reply, "Ummm...I don't think so." I informed them, that if he were six and I was a clown at his birthday party that would be fun but for this type of meeting, my goal is to paint a picture that everyone can see themselves in because that is what teamwork and a work family mentality is all about. They thought for a minute and decided they liked my perspective best!

When the event was over, I got a standing ovation, however the CEO walked right past me and didn't even shake my hand or say, "Thank you." Now, I should point out, I never expect anyone to thank me after my speeches. However, when leaders do, it is impressive because it communicates the vibe of their organization. If you have leadership that looks for reasons to express gratitude and acknowledge when they see someone succeed at their assigned task that is huge. That says they are looking for great things to happen and want them to keep happening.

They are expecting good things to happen and not always assuming the worst is coming.

When you have an attitude of entitlement, basically, it's only a matter of time before things go sideways and they will quickly with that attitude. I have never met anyone that has shared entitlement as their source of success. You need to remember, that a title is not leadership and you do not need a title to be a leader. The number of years and seniority you might have is not what will make you a leader. True leadership is a daily practice. It is a daily choice and an intentional effort. It is a commitment to doing your best while also always elevating what your best is. You should become a better leader next year... even if you have been great. For example, I am an artist and you if look at a painting I did five years ago you might wonder if I am the one who painted it. At the time it was my best work. I was proud of it, people liked it and purchased it and displayed it but because I have been continually practicing, learning, trying new techniques, and intentionally growing my skills my art today is on a completely different level. And my goal is that in five years my art will look completely different than it does today. Obviously, my style will stay consistent, but my ability will not. I learn from other artists every day. I try to learn how they do what they do. I don't want to do what they are doing and copy their work but rather I want to learn how they are doing what they do so that I can utilize that knowledge to paint my own unique paintings. Being a leader means actively watching other leaders and learning from what they are doing—what works and avoiding the things that they are doing that do not work. It is listening to what other people like or do not like about their current leader and taking/implementing the best of what you find. It is reading books, listening to podcasts, seeking out mentors. It is an active process that requires consistency and humility. A looter leader is someone who chooses not to do those things. Someone who firmly believes that "good enough is good enough."

The second event where I was doing a book signing after my speech, there was a line around the room. Everyone wanted more. The vibe was different. Everyone treated me like a guest at the best B&B ever. By the time I left, I was like, "I don't want to go! These people are amazing."

I signed books for nearly an hour and finally, the last person in line stepped up. It was the CEO. He waited in line for an hour to get his book signed and to say those two powerful words that engaging leaders use often, "Thank you!"

This guy was a ROOTER! We talked for a good 10 minutes about family and his grandkids. He kept expressing how grateful he was for the people in his organization. It was nothing short of impressive.

The moral of this chapter is be the best rooter you can be. That is how you cultivate a culture where people are excited to come to work.

Empathy is Your Game Changer

Empathy is the recognition that others have a story. Empathy is offering the gift of compassion, understanding, patience, care, support, and respect. It's not making someone feel judged or out of place because they are experiencing a particular circumstance in their life.

As an engaging leader, you must pay attention to the vibe of your tribe. I know that sounds a little cheesy, but it's true. Most people aren't going to walk into your office and give you their honest feedback or share what they are finding challenging. They won't feel comfortable sharing something that is happening outside of their work life that is making their work life more difficult. And frankly sometimes the details of what they are going through outside of work are not appropriate to share in a workplace environment. But you can still recognize when someone is going through a difficult time without needing to know the specifics of exactly what is happening. Meeting with you should not turn into a therapy session but it should be a time for you to identify different ways you can set that person up for success in their job each day. Many times, you will find there are simple solutions you can offer that will improve both areas of their life. For example, if they are worried about and struggling to be able to leave on time to pick up their kids maybe offer for them to start work an hour earlier so they can leave work an hour early. This way they will not be spending their time at work distracted because they are worried about that, and they will be able to focus and do their best work. It is a win/win for both parties.

Empathy allows people to be authentic, real, and human. It provides safety. If you can't be real, then you are forced to be fake and that is not good. No one thrives when they are working for a leader who is faking their way through the day.

Empathy is how you build loyalty in your organization. If someone feels safe, they tend to lay down roots where they know they are best supported.

Empathy is paying attention and acknowledging someone's story without passing judgment.

PIVOT! PIVOT! PIVOT!

The title of this chapter is what I heard when I played college basketball. My coach would yell, "PIVOT!" and it would echo throughout the gym and in our eardrums. During the pandemic, many of us heard this term for the first time and felt forced into embracing the concept. However, whether you realize it or not, you have been pivoting all along. Things are always changing and with change, we make changes. That is called pivoting.

Here is what I know about change. It is uncomfortable, inconvenient, often expensive, and highly resisted—even if it's good change. But how you embrace change determines how change will work for you. It starts with attitude first.

To pivot in times of change or uncertainty, it doesn't have to be as stressful as we make it out to be. I believe that another way, or the best way, to think of the concept of pivot is to see it for what it really is—an opportunity to be creative and resourceful.

The idea isn't to complain about not having the best of things, but rather choosing an attitude to make the best of things.

The best example I can think of is before the pandemic, our family had planned a big trip to Disney World. Do you want to know one of the most challenging things as a parent—getting your kids excited for a year and then telling them at the last minute it's not happening. Talk about a total buzz kill. I was looking forward to it, too. If you have ever stayed at the Floridian on the Disney properties, you would know I was bummed out as well. That place is amazing!

So, my wife and I came up with a plan. We did the best we could to explain things to the kids, but we also had an opportunity to be creative and resourceful. While, it's not the best of what we wanted, we opted to make the best of it, and that turned out the best.

Instead of going to Disney, we brought Disney to the Glenn Household. For several weeks every Friday night, we picked a Disney theme, picked a movie, decorated the house, and cooked fun food. We all got to pick our favorite Disney theme. Mine was Wreck It Ralph. Which by the way, is a must watch for any great leader. It has such a relevant and meaningful message to the importance of inclusion and recognition.

So instead of going to Disney World for a week, we brought Disney to our home for a month! The kids loved it, and it also gave them something to look forward to during a difficult time. I think when it comes to pivoting, you must do the best you can. You have to try new ideas, some will work and some won't. That is okay, just own it and adjust—more pivots.

To pivot is not something that has to be a bad thing. I have been travelling and speaking at conferences and meetings for over 25 years, so when everything shut down in 2020, I was basically stuck at home. But, instead of complaining about it, I started creating virtual shows that were epic! The best part was I didn't have to travel. Even when everyone started to get Zoomed out, I was creating an experience that made a Zoom or Microsoft Teams meeting exciting. The bottom line, I loved it! My client's loved it! It was a pivot where we all made the best of what wasn't the best.

So, when you are faced with new challenges and know that the only move you have is to pivot, it's best to start with the right attitude and perspective by asking the right questions.

Instead of asking, "WHY did this happen?"

Ask, "HOW can we use this?"

"What can we learn from this?"

"How can we get better from this?"

The right questions will lead you the right solutions. The wrong questions will only create more roadblocks and frustrations.

Ask the people you support daily for their input but understand that not every idea is going to be a champion idea. Be respectful to everyone's input. Some ideas may seem out of left field, but sometimes those are what I call the miracle ideas that change everything for the better. You just never know. Sometimes, you must try things and again, if they work—great! If they don't, keep pivoting.

Quiet Quitting AKA, The Worst Title to a Definition Ever

There is a new term floating around called quiet quitting. The idea behind it is that it's not actually quitting, but rather an employee sets boundaries and doesn't take on additional work outside the scope of their job duties beyond what they are paid to do. Some think of it as not going above and beyond.

Here are my thoughts. I don't think the title fits. It implies that someone is giving up, retreating, or not trying hard. When someone doesn't care or stops putting forth effective effort, that's just called progressive quitting. It is doing less than what is required of them to complete their job duties. It is failing to meet deadlines without expectation, spending more time on their phone than on the tasks at hand, it is coming to work late and then leaving early. In fact, I think progressive quitting isn't all that quiet or hard to identify.

I have read many articles on this subject, and there are a variety of opinions on both ends of the spectrum. Some support it and others do not. As a leader, you should be ahead of the quiet quitting trend and help your people be the most effective in the agreed time frame of work. Just because someone doesn't put in extra hours or take on new projects beyond the scope of their job isn't a bad thing. They are protecting their mental wellbeing, but also trying to have a life. We have three kids at the time of this writing, and time management is everything. We have a framework that structures our time in a way that helps us achieve what we need to get done. Structure is how you budget your time, effort, actions, and attitude in a certain time frame. The moment the structure loses its boundaries is when stress is elevated, things slip through the cracks, and burnout takes over.

I can only speak from the standpoint of an entrepreneur when I share this point, but years ago, when I started hiring for our company, I always laid out the expectations up front. I didn't and still don't care if someone works 10 hours a week or 40 hours a week. All I want is the result. If the work you do gets the desired result, then we are good.

However, if you are over working, that means you are not taking care of yourself. If you are not taking care of your family or yourself, then eventually, you will crash. If your people are set up to crash and burn, it will cost you a fortune.

However, letting them know you care about their well-being and establishing the boundaries with them is a great way to improve engagement. Again, it goes back to the concept, people don't care how much you know, until they know how much you care. If people know you authentically care, they will step up and give less pushback when there is a real need.

Remember, there is a difference between someone who is trying to protect their time by respecting the value of it verse someone who is like, "This place sucks, they don't pay me enough to do extra."

Let me bring this example to light in the next example...

The Red Smock

The best way to highlight this point is an experience that happened to me when I was 18 years old. I had just graduated from high school and got a job working at a gas station convenient store. I wanted to earn extra money before college, so I thought this would be the perfect opportunity.

I call this story, the Red Smock. It involves two different managers. My first manager was awesome. He was kind, approachable, encouraging, engaging, and made going to work worth going to work. The only thing that I didn't like about the job was you were required to wear a red smock. The one I got looked like it had been passed down for centuries without ever being washed. I even took it home and washed it. It only faded the colors, and it didn't look great at all. However, I noticed that my manager always had on a shirt and tie and looked professional. So, I replicated his leadership. I got a shirt and tie, without being asked and started to wear a shirt and tie to work. My manager was impressed. He supported my initiative. However, I should also mention that I felt safe in the environment he created to take that initiative. Have you ever heard an employee say, "I can't do that or I will get in trouble?"

Not in every case, but in most, it indicates employees are not safe to "THINK." They are not safe to think, "What is the best thing to do? What is the right thing to do?"

If you are always worried about getting in trouble for doing what is right or best, that is not a good gig.

So, every day I showed up in a shirt and tie, and I worked. I cleaned bathrooms, the store, restocked shelves, cleaned the parking lot, and helped customers. I was 18 years old, and I felt important and valued. Whenever my manager called to ask if I could come in early, stay late, or do an extra shift, I did it without thinking twice. I had pride in my work and looked forward to it.

A short time later, my super boss got promoted—again. I was so bummed when he left. The new manager was like a train wreck. He didn't care about appearance, and on his first day he told me to take off the tie and put on the red smock. And for the sake of this chapter, let's say right there is when disengagement started. The boundaries of quiet quitting started going up. Mostly because, I didn't like going to work. I did it to get a paycheck. I did what was required of me and no more. When I was asked to stay late, come in early, or do an extra shift—NOPE. It wasn't that I didn't care. I did my best work in the time frame of the job. I just needed to protect my well-being by not being where I wasn't valued, growing, or recognized. My super boss was always recognizing and expressing gratitude for the things that I thought nobody noticed. My new boss was always pointing out everything I did wrong and never noticed anything I did that was good.

The final straw was when my new boss pulled me aside and said, "Sam, if I have to ask you to put on the red smock again, we will have issues."

I realized I was no longer celebrated where I was employed. Time to leave. Did that make me a quitter?

Nope. I didn't like going to work where I was walking on eggshells or afraid of making a mistake. The thought of going to work each day made me feel sick. Nobody should go to a job where they are physically or mentally sick because of stress or poor leadership.

Support the boundaries and well-being of people. Some people can make magic happen in the time frame they have to work. Don't knock it, but rather respect it and support it. I think instead of calling it quiet quitting, we call it working smarter. Also, if you recognize an employee that is consistently having to work extra hours or work beyond the scope of their job to accomplish what you expect from them then you either need to pay them more or hire an additional person to take on some of those responsibilities. If you don't, eventually that person will get burned out and they either start quiet quitting or just outright quit and become an asset to another company. As a leader you have an obligation to hold up your end of the employment agreement they signed when they accepted their position. The "And other duties as assigned" clause in an employment agreement is not a free pass to eventually expect someone to work 50 hours instead of 40 hours a week or take on a huge project well beyond the scope of their normal job duties. If the expectation in your office is that salaried employees actually work 50 hours a week instead of 40, that should be clearly explained and understood before hiring the person. Some people will be totally fine with it, and enjoy it. Some people will have responsibilities outside of work that do not allow them to do that which is also fine. But if that person accepts the job without knowing the expectation, they are being set up to fail. Take the time to think about the actual hours required vs. the salary they are receiving. Those two things need to align or else, again, eventually a person will either get burned out and quit or begin quiet quitting.

Ushy Sushi

The Heart of Excellence

It was late one evening when I was checking into a hotel in downtown Chicago. The desk clerk introduced himself, "Hi, my name is Ushy. How may I help you?"

At first, I thought I heard him say his name wrong, so I responded, "Did you say your name was Sushi?"

"Nope, that's my last name."

"Wait, so your name is Ushy Sushi?"

"Yep."

"Are you kidding?"

"Yep!"

We had a good laugh. Ushy was engaging, pleasant, kind, and helpful. It was nice after a long day. However, my long day was about to get longer. Sometimes with these big hotels, your room may seem like a three day walk to get there from the front desk. So, I made my way to my room with the expectation to get some much-needed rest. When I opened the door, there was someone in there.

"Oops, sorry!"

I journeyed back to the front desk, thinking, "Things happen."

Ushy apologized and got me a new set of keys.

So, I began my hike to the new room. My expectations of rest returned, and the stress started to sift away, until I opened the door. It was a couple and as soon as I stepped in, a woman yelled, "We are being robbed!" And just then, a guy about the size of a NFL Linebacker came flying across the room at me. However, like a Hall of Fame running back, I dodged his take down by closing the door as fast as I could. I heard him bounce off the door. I was in the elevator before he could come out.

I headed to the front desk thinking, "Ushy Sushi is just messing with me."

Now, I am more tired, annoyed, upset, frustrated, and afraid that some guy is now on the hunt looking for me in the hotel.

When I got to the front desk, I calmly said, "Ushy, I am afraid to get a new set of keys from you. Every room you have given me, someone has been in there."

He apologized, got a new set of keys and said, "Let me come with you to make sure everything is okay. As we rode up the elevator, he said something interesting. "Mr. Glenn, I really am sorry. Someone didn't put those rooms as being occupied. The challenge that I face every day is that it is so hard to be your best when others around choose not to be."

You could tell from the moment I arrived; he tried his best. But he had a good point. When someone chooses not to be great, it makes those who are great not look so great.

The point is this before others get better, you must get better and be the example of excellence. Excellence is not complaining about what you do not have, but rather embracing what you do have and making the best of it, while improving.

When you choose to be excellent, you are setting the tone for the standard of service, quality of work, and overall experience. Excellence starts with you.

The Wrap Up!

I am going to borrow Jim Carrey's line from the Movie, ~~Dumb and Dumber~~, "I hate goodbyes!" I know you are busy so if you got to this point, thank you for taking the time to do so. I appreciate that. If I can ever be of service by speaking to your organization or event, please let me know. I have literally one of the best teams in the world... just ask anyone! We all need a little inspiration from time to time to rekindle that SPARK. Just visit, www.SamGlenn.com. Also, if you are looking for videos to show your team to keep them engaged, inspired, and encourage, we are always adding new videos to my video vault on my website.

The idea of this book was and is to encourage you where you are right now. Maybe there is a good spark in your organization already, so the mission is to keep feeding the flame. Keep doing what works. Keep improving. Keep getting better.

On the flip side, maybe there is a missing spark where you are and so it simply means, you have an opportunity to make some new edits to the game plan that improves your culture. Start small and build.

Remember, the goal was to find one good idea in this book that you can implement now. I hope you found that and more.

Also, I love great stories! If you have a story about what is working in your organization, an experience, or need some encouraging suggestions, email us: Contact@SamGlenn.com. We are always happy to help.

Wishing you wellness,

Sam Glenn

Meet the Author

Sam Glenn

Sam Glenn is an award-winning motivational speaker, best selling author, and performance artist. Organizations and leadership teams utilize Sam's uplifting and artistic speeches to recognize, reward, and reinforce effort, attitude, and achievement. Audiences laugh, learn, and experience a moment to recharge and feel good about who they are and what they do.

At one time Sam was negative, depressed, and sleeping nights either in his car or on borrowed floor space. It was a good friend over a cup of coffee, that gave Sam what he calls, "A Kick in the Attitude!" Sam realized that everything follows attitude and that if he wanted his life to change, he needed to start by changing his attitude.

For more than 27 years, Sam has captivated audiences of all sizes, including stadium events up to 75,000 people. Also, Sam's late mentor was the legendary Zig Ziglar.

Today, Sam gives more than 100 speeches a year, working with organizations and leadership teams who really care about the well-being of their people.

To book Sam Glenn to speak at your next event, visit:

www.SamGlenn.com

Or Email Sam's booking team,

Contact@SamGlenn.com

Made in the USA
Monee, IL
23 October 2022

16425171R00066